The Three Wishes

by Dale Lundberg
illustrated by Remy Simard

Harcourt
SCHOOL PUBLISHERS

Printed in China

ISBN 10: 0-15-350979-1
ISBN 13: 978-0-15-350979-7

Ordering Options
ISBN 10: 0-15-350601-6 (Grade 4 On-Level Collection)
ISBN 13: 978-0-15-350601-7 (Grade 4 On-Level Collection)
ISBN 10: 0-15-357932-3 (package of 5)
ISBN 13: 978-0-15-357932-5 (package of 5)

4 5 6 7 8 9 10 0940 12 11 10 09

One day after school, the twins, Mateo and Anita, were playing in the park while their mother read nearby. Usually, they skated and biked on the path that led around the playground. That day, however, they had inadvertently gone the other way on the path. It took them to places they had never seen before.

One of the new places was a small, circular, stone wall with a little roof on top. Anita and Mateo peered down into this unusual structure.

"There is water inside," Anita said.

"I think it's a well!" exclaimed Mateo.

"Maybe it's a wishing well," said Anita. "Quick, let's throw in a penny and see what happens."

The twins dropped the coin into the well and they heard a splash and the sound of chimes. Then they watched in wonder as the water began to bubble, and a cloud of mist rose up from the surface. The mist rose higher and higher and finally, it flowed over the walls of the well. Anita and Mateo stepped back.

"Hello, children," said a soft, gentle voice. "Are you ready to make a wish?"

"Oh, my!" cried Mateo. "It *is* a wishing well!"

"Yes, I am a wishing well and I can grant you three wishes." the voice replied.

Mateo and Anita were in shock because they could not believe their good luck.

Mateo exclaimed, "This is the chance of a lifetime!"

"It may be," cautioned the well. "On the other hand, it may not be as great as it seems. Remember to wish very carefully, because some wishes don't turn out the way you think they will."

"I'll need a moment to talk this over with my sister," Mateo said.

The twins huddled together to talk about their wishes. As Mateo and Anita whispered together, they thought about the vast opportunities they now had before them. "What do you think we should wish for?" each asked the other.

Anita knew what she wanted because she was nervous about a big test that she had to take tomorrow. "How about if we wish that we never have to go to school again?" Anita suggested.

"That's a great wish," Mateo agreed. "Let's save the other two for later."

The excited twins returned to the well. Drawing himself up to his full stature, Mateo announced, "We wish that we never have to go to school again."

A sound like a sigh came from the bottom of the well and the voice said, "It never fails. Most people have good intentions, but few choose their wishes carefully. All the same, I grant your wish. Good luck with it."

Mateo and Anita were as happy as could be. No more school, ever! Then they heard their mother calling them.

The next morning, there was no relentless ringing of the alarm clock and the twins' parents did not wake them. Finally, Anita woke up, leaped out of bed, and ran to Mateo's room.

"Hey, Mateo! It worked!" she cried. "We didn't have to go to school today!"

For the rest of the day, the twins did whatever they wanted. They colored, read, and worked on a big jigsaw puzzle that they had never had time for before. No one said a word about school and it went on that way for a week.

Each day, they got out of bed whenever they wanted, they played all day and they did not have to do any homework. It seemed too good to be true.

However, by the time the next Monday rolled around, the twins realized that they were bored. They decided to go to the schoolyard during lunchtime to visit their friends and catch up on the latest news.

When they arrived, the twins saw all their friends playing, running, shouting, and laughing. The children at school were having a great time. Anita and Mateo ran to the gate, but they could not get in.

Mateo and Anita walked away sadly. All their friends were in school and there was no one to play with.

"I think we made a mistake, Mateo," said Anita. "Let's go back to the wishing well."

Anita and Mateo went back to the park with their mother. While she got settled, Anita and Mateo headed straight for the well. Anita peered down to the water as Mateo dropped in a coin. As it had before, the water began to bubble, the mist rose up, and the wind chimes sounded.

"Hello, Mateo and Anita, how's the wish working out?" said the voice.

Anita answered, "Wishing Well, we think we made a mistake and we want to make our second wish."

"Wishing Well," said Mateo, "we wish to go back to school."

"Good choice, children. I grant your second wish," said the well.

The next day, Mateo and Anita were happy to be back in school. True, Anita had missed the test, but they had missed some fun things, too. They had missed a painting project, a sing-along session and mostly being with their friends. Both children agreed that their second wish was better than their first.

That afternoon, as the twins were doing their homework, they began to talk about their third wish. "What should we wish for?" asked Anita.

"I'm not sure," said Mateo. "We know that we need to be careful because this wishing business is harder than it seems."

Back at the park the next day, their mother told them not to go far. The children went over to the well, where it was Anita's turn to drop in the coin. Once again, the water bubbled, the mist rose, and the chimes sounded.

"How's the second wish coming along?" asked the soft voice.

"It's going very well," said Mateo. "However, we're not sure what to do with our third wish. Wishing Well, do you have an idea?"

"Yes, I do. You see, I, too, have a wish," said the Wishing Well.

This answer roused the twins' curiosity. "You *do*?" asked Mateo. "Well, what is your wish?"

The well answered, "For a long time now, I have wished to be a river. All this time, I have only been able to help and teach people who came to me. If I were a bountiful river, I am sure that I could help more people. Besides, I have always wanted to see the world."

Mateo and Anita looked at each other and nodded. It made sense to use their last wish to help the wishing well.

"Wishing Well," they said together. "You are resourceful and wise. Our wish is that you should be a river."

As soon as the twins spoke, they heard the sound of running water behind them. A lovely river that the twins had never noticed before was flowing through the park. Their mother was reading beside it, and it looked like the river had always been there. Anita and Mateo looked at each other and smiled.

"Enjoy your wish, Wishing Well!" Anita called. The river sparkled in answer. Mateo and Anita decided that their last wish had been the best one of all.

Think Critically

1. How do you know that this story is a fantasy? What other fantasy stories have you read?

2. When did you begin to think that Mateo and Anita had made a poor choice for their first wish?

3. What do you think is the moral of this story?

4. What are some other words that have the same meaning as *vast* does on page 6?

5. If you were Anita or Mateo, what would you have wished for?

 ## Language Arts

Write and Draw Write a different ending for the story, beginning with Anita and Mateo's third wish. Draw pictures to illustrate your new ending.

School-Home Connection Share this story with a family member. Then talk about things you would each wish for if you had the chance.

Word Count: 1,180